By April's Kiss

David Di Paolo

By April's Kiss, Published March, 2017

Cover Art: Diane Ditzler Frossard
Interior Layout and Cover Design: Howard Johnson
Editorial & Proofreading: Eden Rivers Editorial Services; Karen Grennan

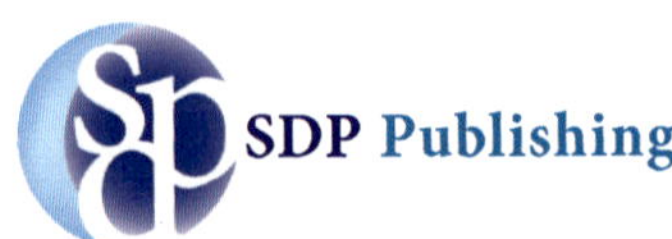

Published by SDP Publishing, an imprint of SDP Publishing Solutions, LLC.

For more information about this book contact Lisa Akoury-Ross at SDP Publishing by e-mail at info@SDPPublishing.com.

ISBN-13 (print): 978-0-9981277-4-3
ISBN-13 (ebook): 978-0-9981277-5-0

Library of Congress Control Number: 2016960042

Printed in the United States of America

Dedication

For my father

and

for Grace

Foreword

By April's Kiss comprises a series of reflections and descriptive passages, accompanied by photographs and artwork. This compilation was a product of two major life events that came on the heels of one another: my father's sudden and untimely passing, and a personal diagnosis of early stage cancer. The piece is in three parts, which are grouped by mood: By the Creek, In the Cave, and In the Meadow. Some of the earlier entries reflect a period during which I sought solitude and the lonely comfort of night. My hope is that the life-affirming poems in the third section will resonate with those who have experienced similar emotions: confronted with the death of a loved one, a diagnosis of cancer, or any other of life's challenges that send us in search of solace, encouragement, and personal discovery.

I envision this work much like a concept album in the days of classic rock and progressive rock music—in the vein of *Sergeant Pepper's Lonely Hearts Club Band* by the Beatles, *Thick as a Brick* by Jethro Tull, or *Brain Salad Surgery* by Emerson, Lake & Palmer—being unified by thematic content and meant to be experienced in one sitting, in about one hour (and hopefully worthy of repeat reads).

There are perhaps two pieces that require context. "Wonder" hearkens back to the beguilement I felt as a teenage schoolboy, staring out the window from an isolated cabin in the Pocono mountains, daydreaming, with the prep school's summer reading assignment of George Steinbeck's *The Acts of King Arthur and His Noble Knights* laying open on the pillow in front of me. My cross-country bunk mate, John, introduced me to the recently released *Rumours* album by Fleetwood Mac, letting the vinyl disc spin incessantly for the several-hour break between our morning and evening runs, and carefully resetting the phonograph needle to "Dreams" (the album's second track), after "Gold Dust Woman" would fade into silence. Before the weeklong camp ended, there was a moment when I gazed out the window and conjured a vision of Stevie Nicks singing in the woods, twirling in delight to the melody. It is one of those enchanting memories that remains in my mind decades later, as vivid as if it happened yesterday. It was an early experience of the power of music, as well as a blissful synthesis of fantasy and reality.

"Cursed" draws its inspiration from *Cat People*, the classic 1942 noir horror film by Val Lewton, starring Simone Simon as the tragic heroine Irena, who is haunted by a lifelong curse. Irena has fled from her past in a remote Serbian village to New York City. She has resigned herself to the conviction that her soul is forever lost; the best she can hope to achieve with her life is to suppress the evil hidden inside her and prevent herself from transforming into a black panther that will kill anyone who causes her jealousy or anger. She cheerily observes to the man she will marry that she likes the dark. "It's friendly."

So, with that, let me lead you to the bank of Neshaminy Creek in Tyler State Park, or beside a small trickling stream in a quiet place of your choice....

Table of Contents

3 *In the Meadow* 47

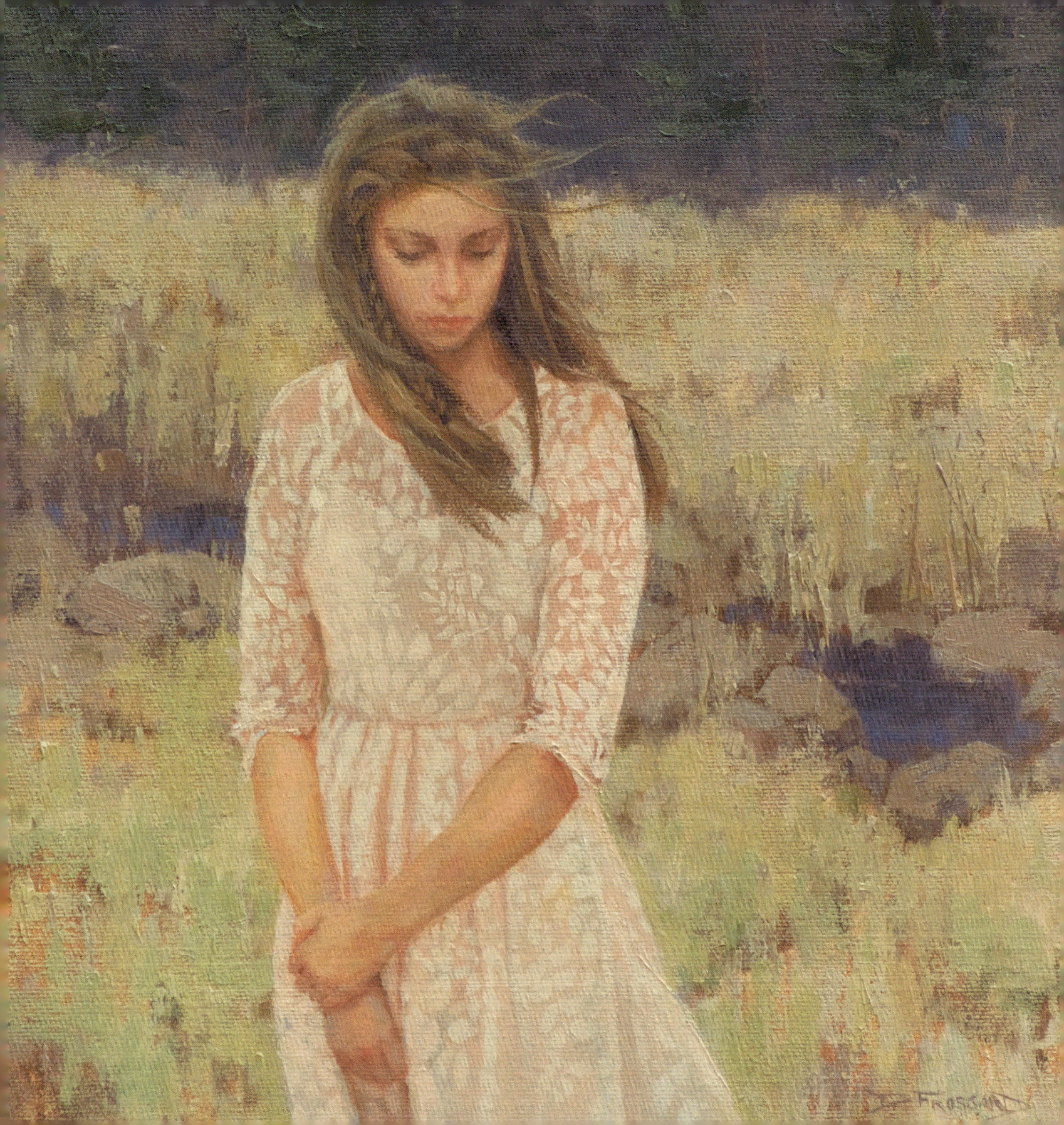
FROSSARD

1

By the Creek

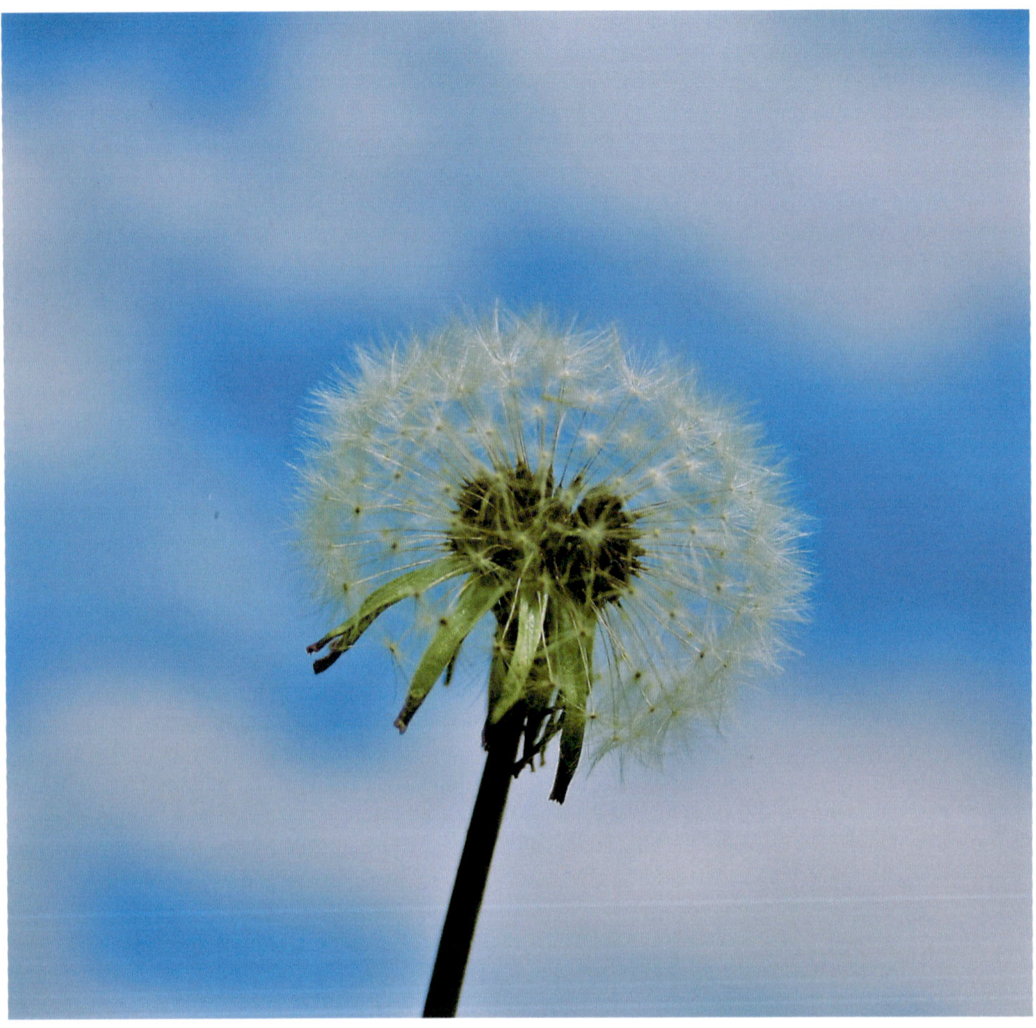

The Nomad

I was a seed
blown from far away,
on dandelion wings,
by April's kiss.

My roots, they've yearned
for the arable fields
of a distant land,
so long forlorn.

Legs I've grown,
in search of the place
where I know I belong:
The home I should have called my own.

In the alpine meadow
where the daisies dance
and the heather sings,
while the lazy glacial melt
slowly bids farewell
to the shape-shifting clouds
pantomiming fairy tales.

For now,
I must be content
to be a nomad
drifting through vacuous space,
lost in time's folds,
always seeking that greener place.

New Moon

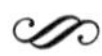

Spin.
Spin the yarn, miller's daughter.
Tell your tale.
Withhold not a trifle;
turn your straw into gold.

Scrub.
Scrub the floor, Cinderella.
Wash away your tears;
mind your tongue as you trim your sisters' gowns.

Wander.
Wander the woods, Goldilocks,
until Wonderland you find.
Take Alice by her hand and hasten home.

Tick, tock, tick—
The rabbit's watch sounds the alarm.
Sun set,
moon arise.

The day is coming …
it's almost here.

The villagers are gathering
to secure the gate.
Thought banished from their psyche all of you were;
no longer had they need of legends and fables.

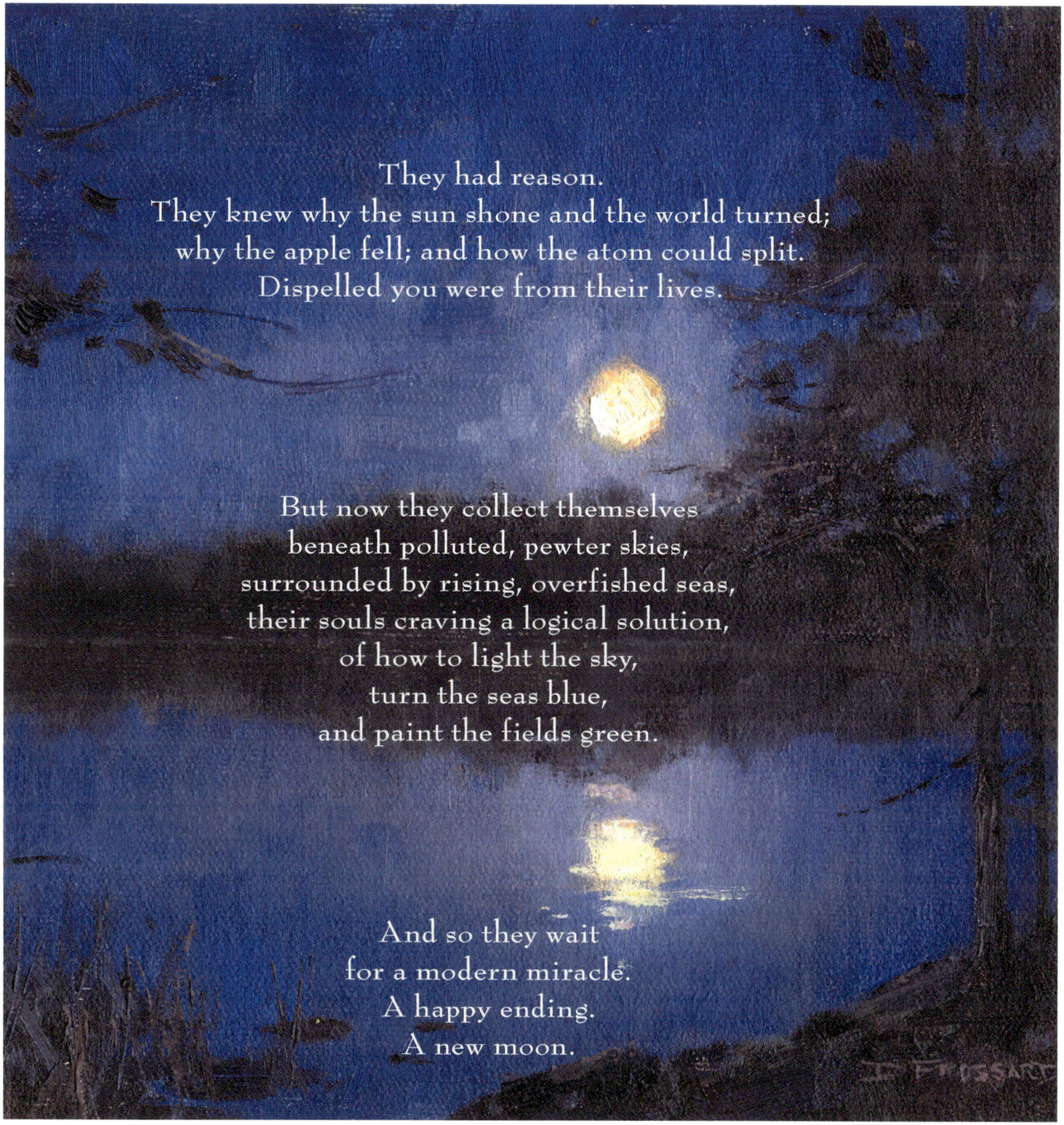

They had reason.
They knew why the sun shone and the world turned;
why the apple fell; and how the atom could split.
Dispelled you were from their lives.

But now they collect themselves
beneath polluted, pewter skies,
surrounded by rising, overfished seas,
their souls craving a logical solution,
of how to light the sky,
turn the seas blue,
and paint the fields green.

And so they wait
for a modern miracle.
A happy ending.
A new moon.

The Fog

The fog.
I can feel it.
It's alive.
Suckled by my insecurities
and sorrow.
It billows with my angst,
clouds my vision,
encircles and binds me.

I can't escape him.
Can you?

He's reaching out.
He's tapping you on the shoulder,
whispering,
"My name is ______."

Wandering Disillusion

To raise a fire,
only to be overpowered by its smoke;
to trace the footpath,
and then to discover the thicket;
to tender the carrot,
yet the rabbit snubs past.

Boots submerged to the ankle,
moored by the suction of the muddy bank.
My gaze is caught by the floating driftwood
tumbling over the failing dam,
spinning in confusion
and disintegrating downstream.

The loud plop
as I extricate my foot
sends the sunning turtles
diving deep from the moss-painted rocks.

The deep footprint
records my presence;
a testimony to survive many storms.
Yes, I was here.

In the creek,
the geese assemble.
Taking respite from their autumnal journey,
they cool the webbing of their feet
and rest their tired wings.

As they share their honking tales,
in a convivial gathering,
I imagine that I might join
in the fellowship.

Spying my approach,
the flock voices their disillusion of my kind,
born of their wanderings.

Ire of the forlorn and outcast hunter raised,
the bow is leveled,
after the fingers have retracted
the straightest of arrows from the quiver.

Their suspicions confirmed,
the birds launch into the clouds,
leave me in a daze,
amidst the shedding trees.

The wind echoes the call of Lenape brethren,
long departed from this place.
Their arrowheads I find,
and amidst shards of an old wigwam—
that somehow have managed to survive
the passage of centuries—
I dig a hole
and bury these mementos.

I stare at the earth
and envision the footprints of a legion
chased away from their homeland.

Their imprints seem to match mine.
I follow their trail,
but the path abruptly ends,
leaving me in wandering disillusion.

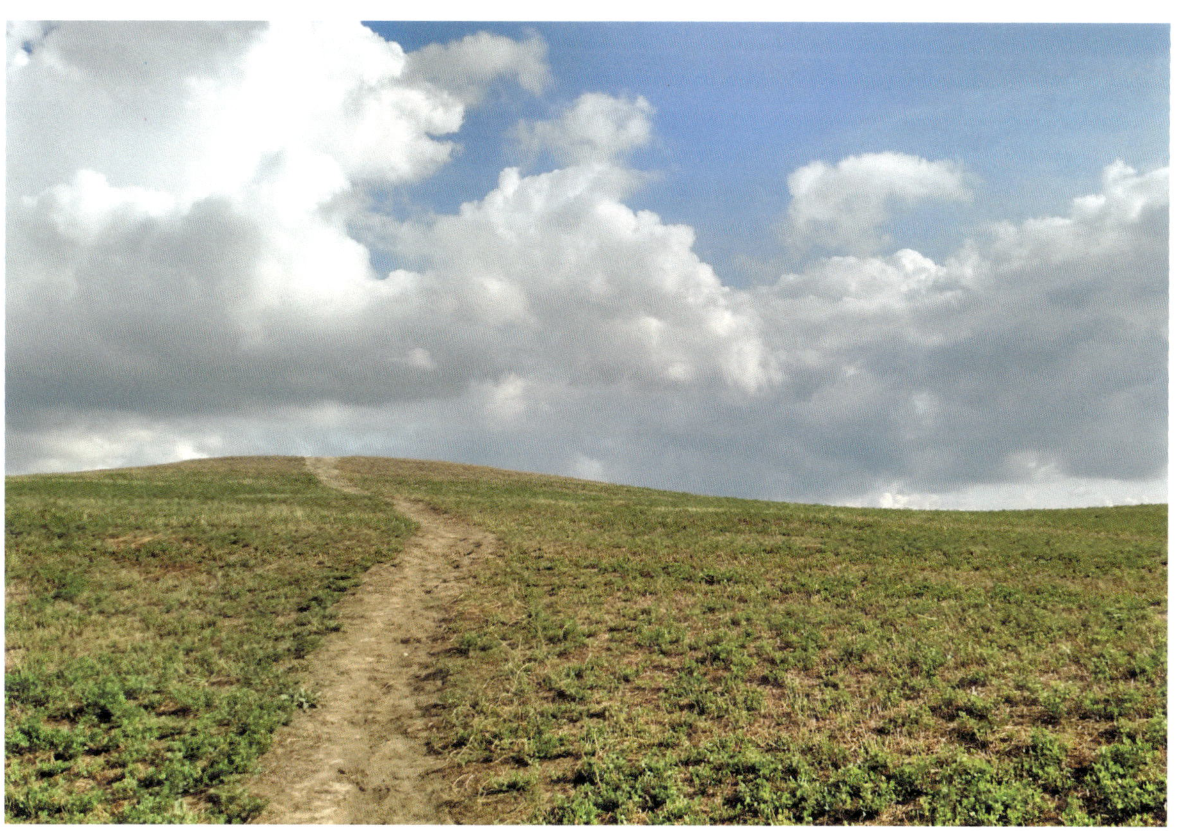

Succession

What will you learn today?
What flower will you pluck?
What insect will entrance?
What color of crayon excites?

With delight and anticipation you awake
to the call of your teacher:
the dawn.

What places will you find?
What name will you learn?
What face will make you smile?
What memories will you store
in the growing awareness of your mind?

What discoveries await,
on this first leg of your journey,
when every port is new,
and every breeze that fills your sails is as fresh as the dew,
when songs make you sing,
and the littlest excitement
makes you dance?
Laughter is your guide
through the seas you begin to chart.

Where has the time gone?
It seems like you just departed.
The wind is empty;
the canvas doused.
The ship but sways back and forth.

What will you forget today?
What smile will vanish?
What name will evade?
What face will shed its identity?
What fragrance no longer can you place?
What precious nook have you forgotten?
What vivid memory has now grayed into obscurity—
never to return?
And what is the thought that you can't get out of your head,
as you lose track of time,
and aimlessly drift?

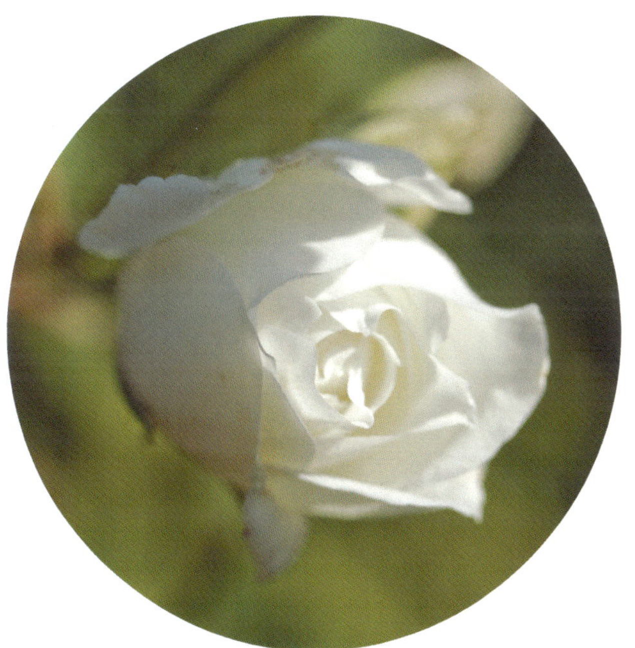

The Ghost Boy

The chill of your disembodied whisper
fills the canal in my ear, calling,
“Daddy!”
Your familiar greeting wakes me
in the still of the night
to the faithful display
of my bedside clock:
“3:30.”

How long has your spirit roamed this house?
Retreading old ground?
Are you looking for your special box,
with your rabbit’s foot, your painted rock
(and other prized objects),
that you hid under the bed?

I glimpse your diminutive shadow,
eclipsing the nightlight,
as you traverse the hallway.
You’re not looking for me,
but I cannot say the same for myself.
In your shadow,
there is mystery,
a reality kept hidden from me
by my own mind.
You always will be
the vision that eludes me.
My discarnate childhood soul.

What I'm Not

I'm a place not a person;
a concept not a place;
a word not a concept;
a thing not a word;
a movement not a thing;
a dance not a movement;
a song not a dance;
a feeling not a song;
a fire not a feeling;
the sky not a fire;
the sea not the sky;
the forest not the sea;
the mountain not the forest;
just a rock not a mountain.

No, I think or just feel
that I'm something between fluid and solid,
less certain than shifting sand.
I'm not sure what I am;
I'm only sure what I'm not.

Dear John

Thank you for the music.
Thank you for the thoughts.
At a time of searching,
a compass you brought.

You vocalized your visions.
You lyricized your dreams.
Of a world of peace,
of harmony and song.

Imagine there's a heaven—
I wonder if you can,
a world of purpose,
values transcending man.

Follow me past the poppies,
through a young man's idealistic field.

Discover a cave,
whose void is shining.
Surrender to the solitude,
from where why can be found.

The evidence compelling;
probability close to one.
The legions of molecules,
in a life-producing dance,
tell the tale for what it is.
The instructions are not random,
and you are not a concept
by which pain is measured.
But why does the planet feel so alone?

Imagine if you will:
one another.
Imagine if you will:
a family.
Imagine if you can:
as good as it can possibly be—
the future.

Groundhogs

The clouds thicken.
The blue evaporates.
Dragonflies retreat across the creek
when we emerge,
each from our impressive burrows.
We may look alike to you.
We may seem to commune,
but loners are we, all.

The day's tasks must be done.
All of this greenery must be consumed.
Nibble, swallow,
nibble, swallow.
So busy,
barely moving,
we rise up on our hind legs
at the doe's approach.

Toiling down the list,
before the sun departs,
There is no time—
to be cooled by the autumnal breeze,
to discover the trail behind the pines,
to shudder in the November morning mist,
to swim in the brisk, crackling waters,
a stone's throw from the hovels we deem splendid.

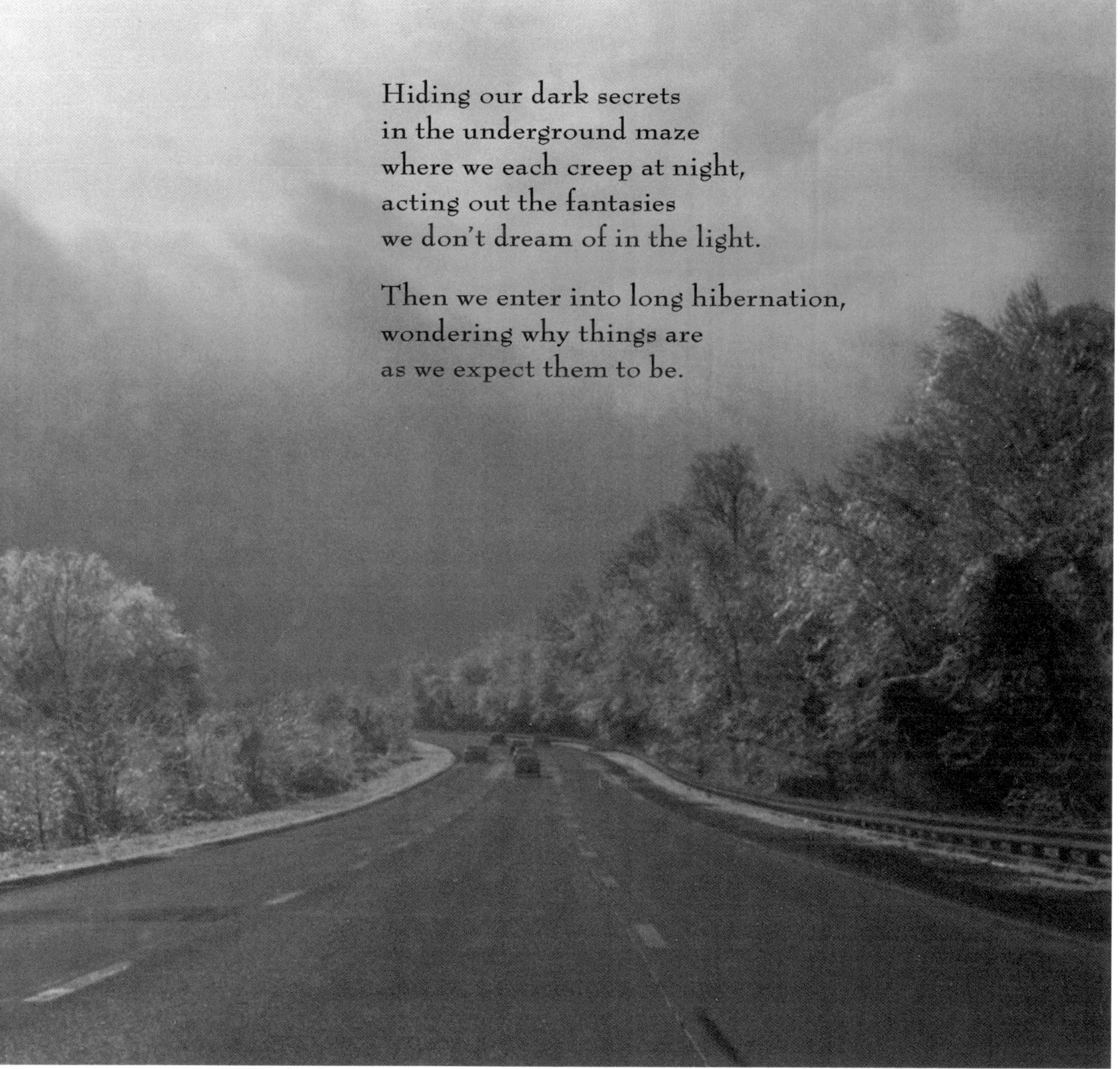

Hiding our dark secrets
in the underground maze
where we each creep at night,
acting out the fantasies
we don't dream of in the light.

Then we enter into long hibernation,
wondering why things are
as we expect them to be.

Faith

I am on a quest for a vision—
a miracle.
I wait in hope,
gazing at each sunset
from the hill above the creek,
beneath a canopy of oaks and sycamores,
waiting as the crows caw
and the creek water crackles.
The firefly concert commences,
a glowing, golden song
filling the breeze,
while in the distance,
the fiery orange orb kisses the horizon.

I cannot tell you what I expect—
only that I will know the miracle for what it is,
when it finally arrives.
It is on its way.
One day.

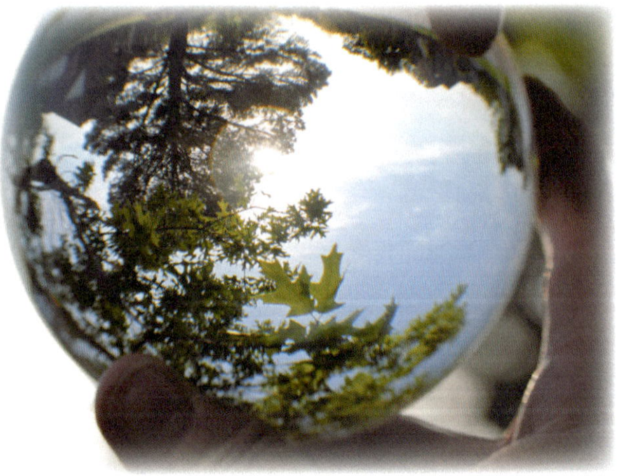

Hive

We're beyond that.
Hatred.
We're beyond that.

Prejudice.
We're beyond that.

War and mistrust?
We're beyond that.

Religion, superstition, faith?
We're beyond them.

Hope—beyond it.

DNA?
We're beyond that.

Atomic bomb,
space travel,
time capsules,
cancer,
resurrection,
relativity,
alchemy,
Grand Unified Theory,
suspended animation,
spontaneous combustion,
global warming?
We're beyond it all.

We are a hive.
An asocial hive:
That's all there is.
That's all that remains.

Individual ambitions:
Put them aside,
and enter the hive.

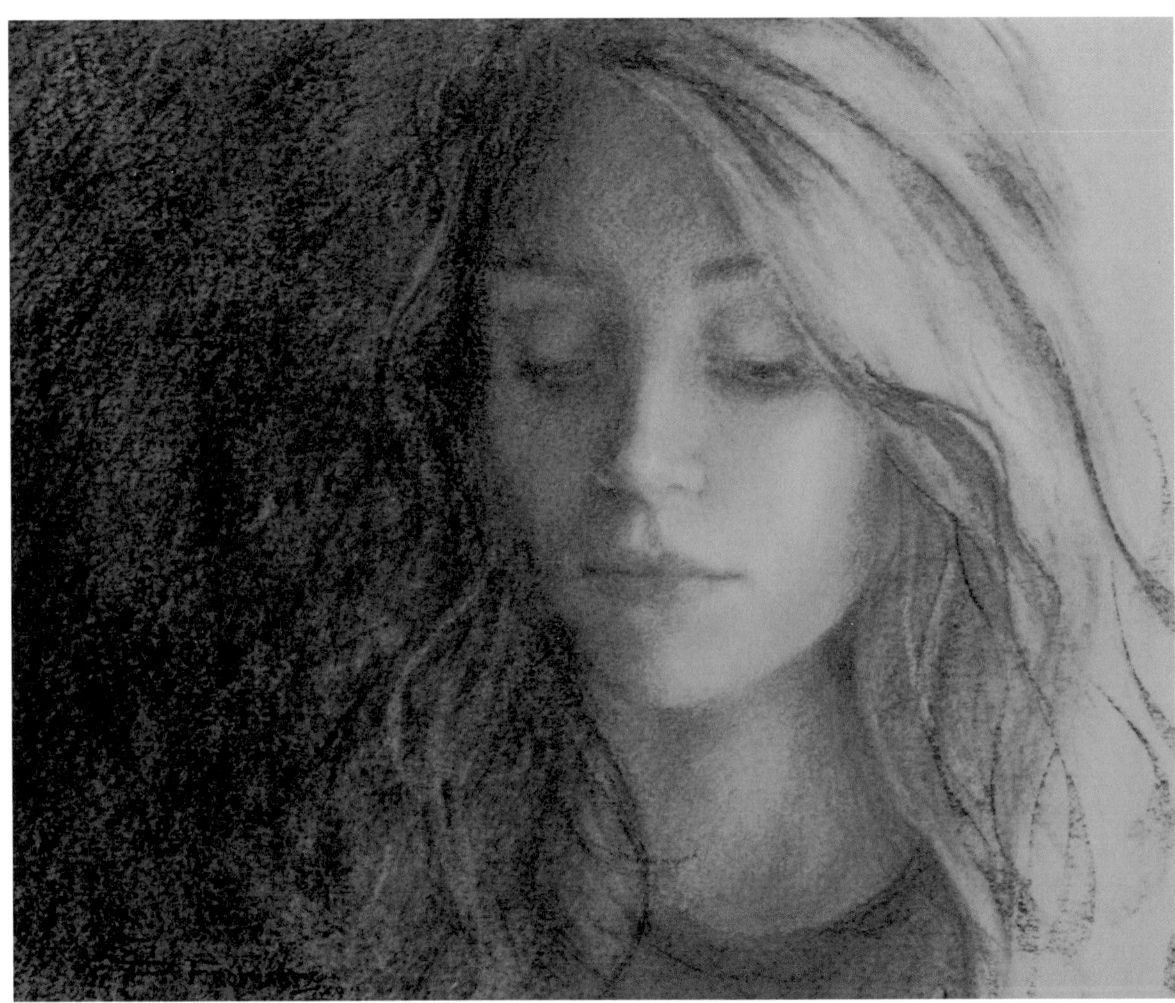

2

In the Cave

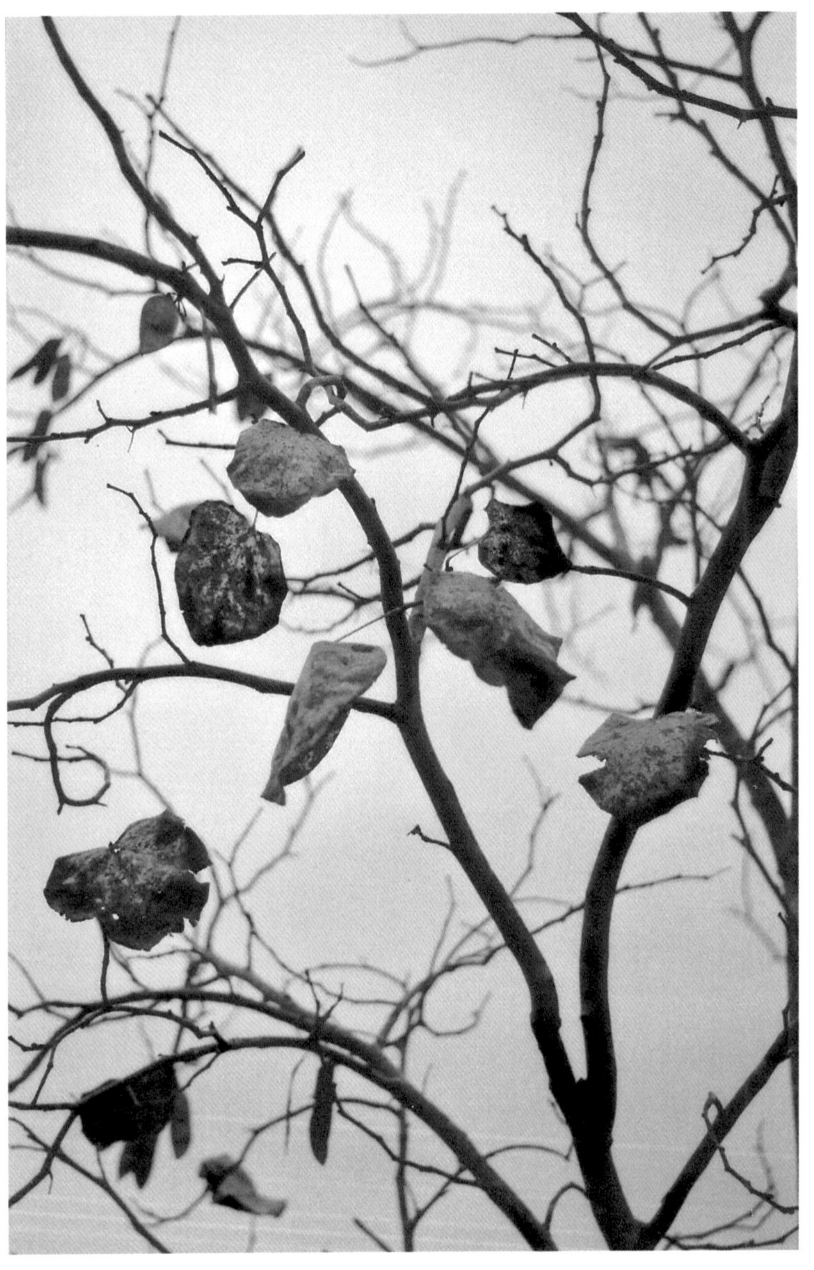

Grayness

I am the grayness of the world
the fog
the blur
the lens that doesn't focus

I am the grayness of the world
the parable without a moral
plan devoid of purpose
aimless motion

drift with me
on a predictable orbit
beneath the overcast skies
clinging to the middle of the flat, white road

The Fig Tree

Beyond the veranda,
inside the walls
of the place I call home
stands a defiant tree.

Your curling fronds
that were caressed
by the summer breeze
refuse to unfurl.

You have been immune
to the nourishment of the soil
that swaddled you;
no drink did you take
of the water showered on you.

Did the sun I not give you?
Did the rain I not bestow upon you?
Did I not prune you and groom you?
And nurse you whenever you ailed?

Yet what did you return to me?
Your fruit withers and drops.
Barrenness is your fancy,
a life of spite
that you display, like regalia,
relishing my chagrin.

I do grant
one last chance
to unfurl your fronds,
to bask in the sun,
to throw forth your shade,
and bud with pride and generosity.

For if I didn't love you as I did,
all I could do would be to curse you.
Even now, I hesitate.
But what is a gardener to do?

Beyond the veranda
inside the walls
of the place I call home …
stands a defiant tree.

Fog II

The fog,
he's found me again.
I tried to hide,
but he's like my shadow,
or a conjoined twin.
If only I could sever our bond,
and douse his darkness
with a bucket of light.

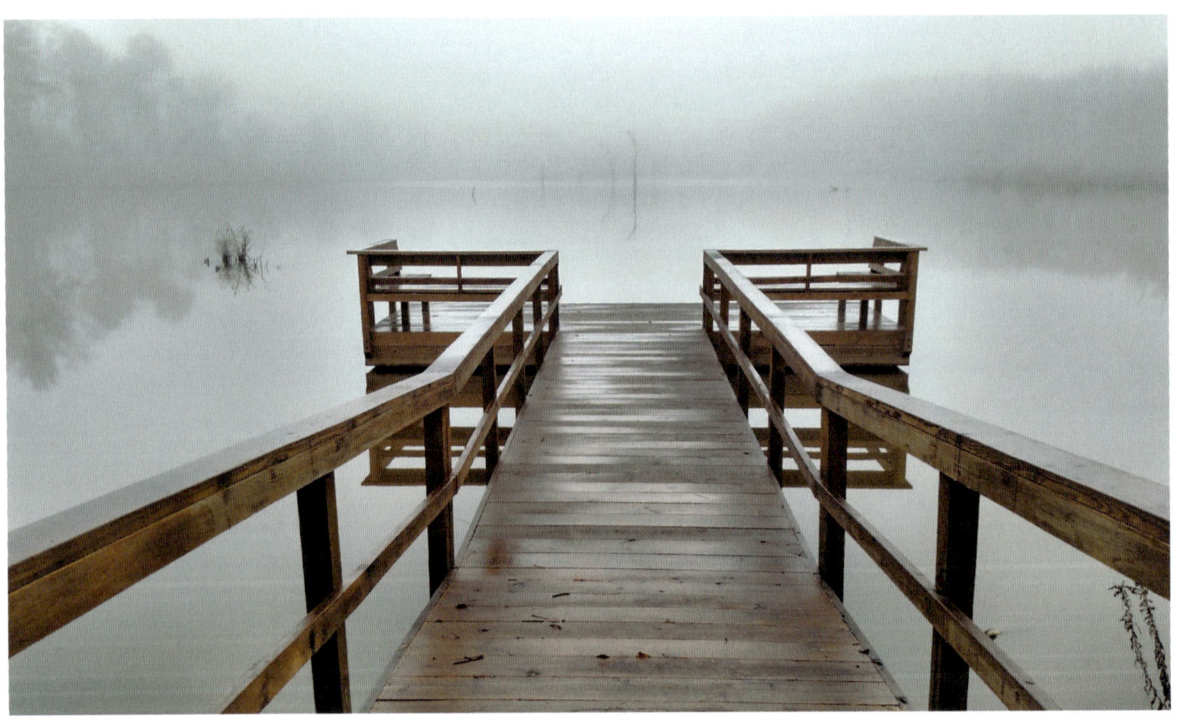

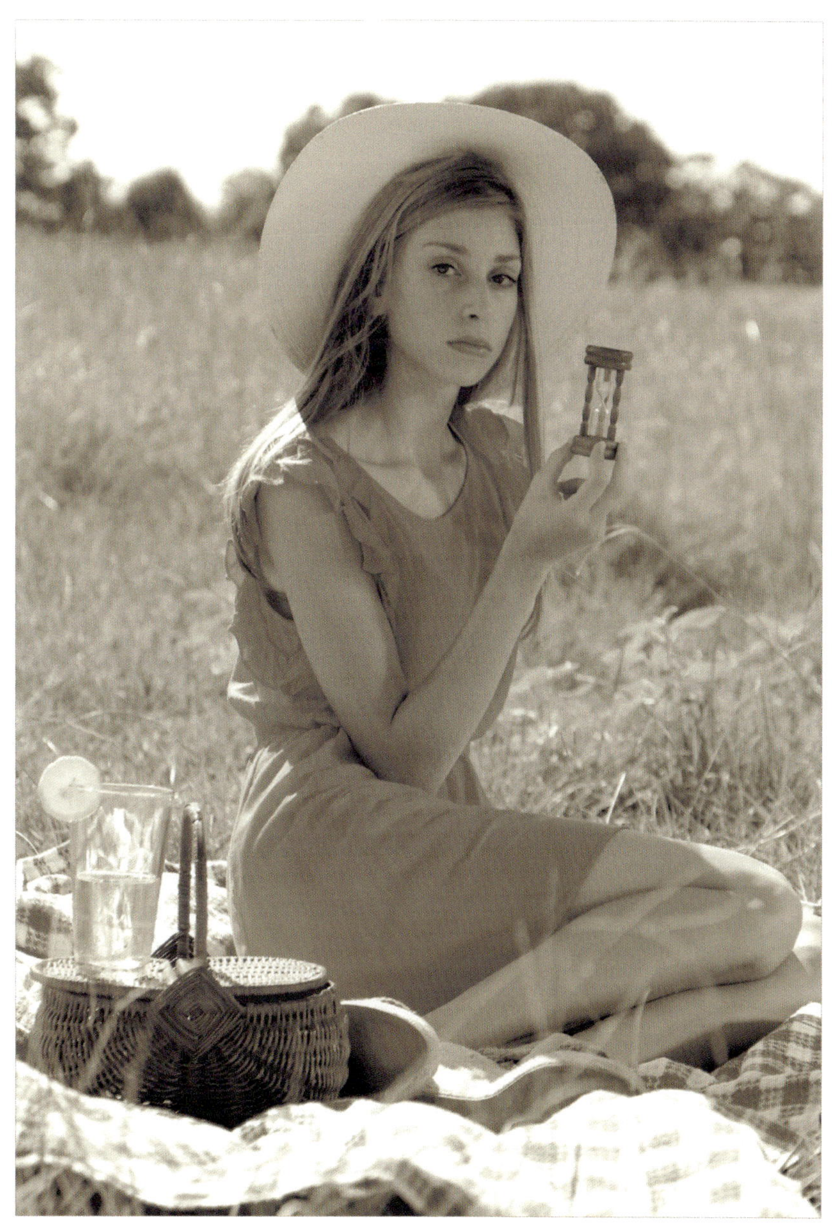

The Lemon Tree

Who would be so bold
as to crave your bitter fruit?
Armed with bloodthirsty thorns,
you covet what little you possess—
sour essence in its thick cocoon.

Thought yourself so powerful,
impenetrable,
smug in your potency.

But your defenses are flawed,
your mission has failed,
for I have stolen what you hold so dear—
squeezed its vitality,
slurped its juice.

Never will I relent.
No quarter will I grant.
No pardon expect.
No mercy will you be given.

Ingénue you misread me.
Behold! I have grown stronger
than you ever could have imagined,
and now I am the potentate—
the seer and overseer—
of all of the bounty
in this garden.

O duplicitous one,
I will succeed where you have fallen,
for this is my time,

my turn to reign....

And the snake continued to wriggle beneath the woman's feet,
unaware of the cherry blossoms about to bud,
and the child about to be born.

I Will Miss

The smell of lavender
and a Lincoln rose;
the light that fires the August sunset;
the syrupy smell of November puddles
in the sugar maple forest.

Dispatching the dandelion seeds of the parachute balls,
with a slow, steady wind born deep inside my chest.
Waking to the morning coffee brewing itself in the kitchen.
My stomach lifting with a thrill,
as the swing rushes back to Earth.

Running through Tyler Park
and steady April showers;
faltering on the mossy rock,
while the crows overhead caw in indifference,
and the mist conceals the trail ahead.

The geese flying in tight formation,
the muddy grove long forgotten,
the anticipation of Christmas morning,
the golden hour of the evening sun,
lighting a Tuscan field and a Napa vineyard;
the coastal redwoods of Armstrong,
the whipping winds of Jenner Beach,
sandblasting the skin from my cheeks.
The satisfying feel of my Pentax,
and the pinch harmonics on my Ibanez.

The deep-throated hoot of the great horned owl,
clutching the antenna
on the roof of the split-level across Andrea Drive,
waiting under the full moon
at 4:00 a.m.,
for a furry creature to emerge from under the snowball bush,
its voice calling from beneath my bedroom window,
lifted 6 inches above the sill.

Shivering in the bed,
while the January wind whistles through the gaps,
around the frame of the builder-grade window,
on the verge of splintering
in a lonely room in a suburb deep in its slumber.

How good it was to shiver!

All these moments of solitude
I will miss.
All these moments I never shared,
nay only with my siblings: the foliage and the animals,
who speak not a word.

If I have a spirit that lives on,
I will miss these things,
these things I kept to myself.

Cursed

My soul is lost
within a dark forest,
and I have no peace.

My life has been torment,
suppressing the inner evil.
The curse.
My nature.
My chagrin.

You professed your love
and then betrayed me.
I never intended
to return your affection.

It was my longing
and mystery
that lured you.

But now I can no longer contain my emotions,
nor leash the anger,
the jealousy,
and the craving for revenge.

Existence was damnation.
The soft treading of the cat's feet
always whispering to me.

Fate has arrived:
The claws poke through my skin
and find the light of dark;
ebony tail sprouts,
and sharp fangs emerge.
Blood is what I thirst.

It's an escape into fantasy,
and it's dangerous.
It's an escape into fantasy,
and it's dangerous.

I reject the words of warning.
Destiny must be fulfilled.
I pull open the cage door,
and loose the panther,
setting myself free.

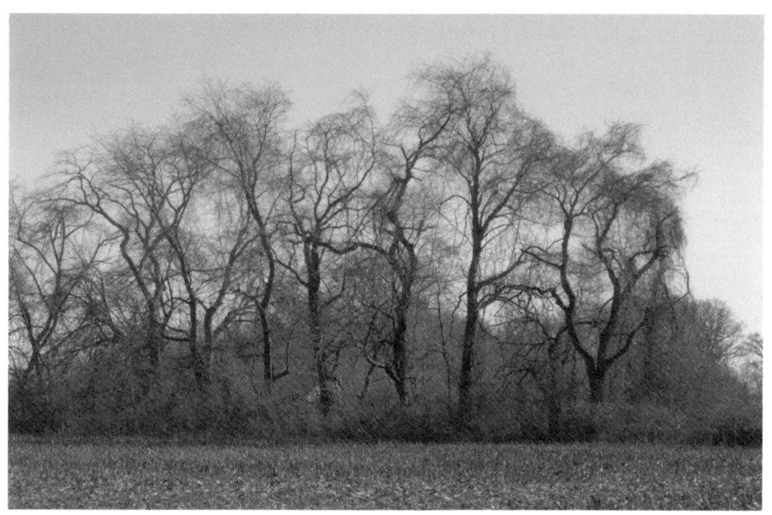

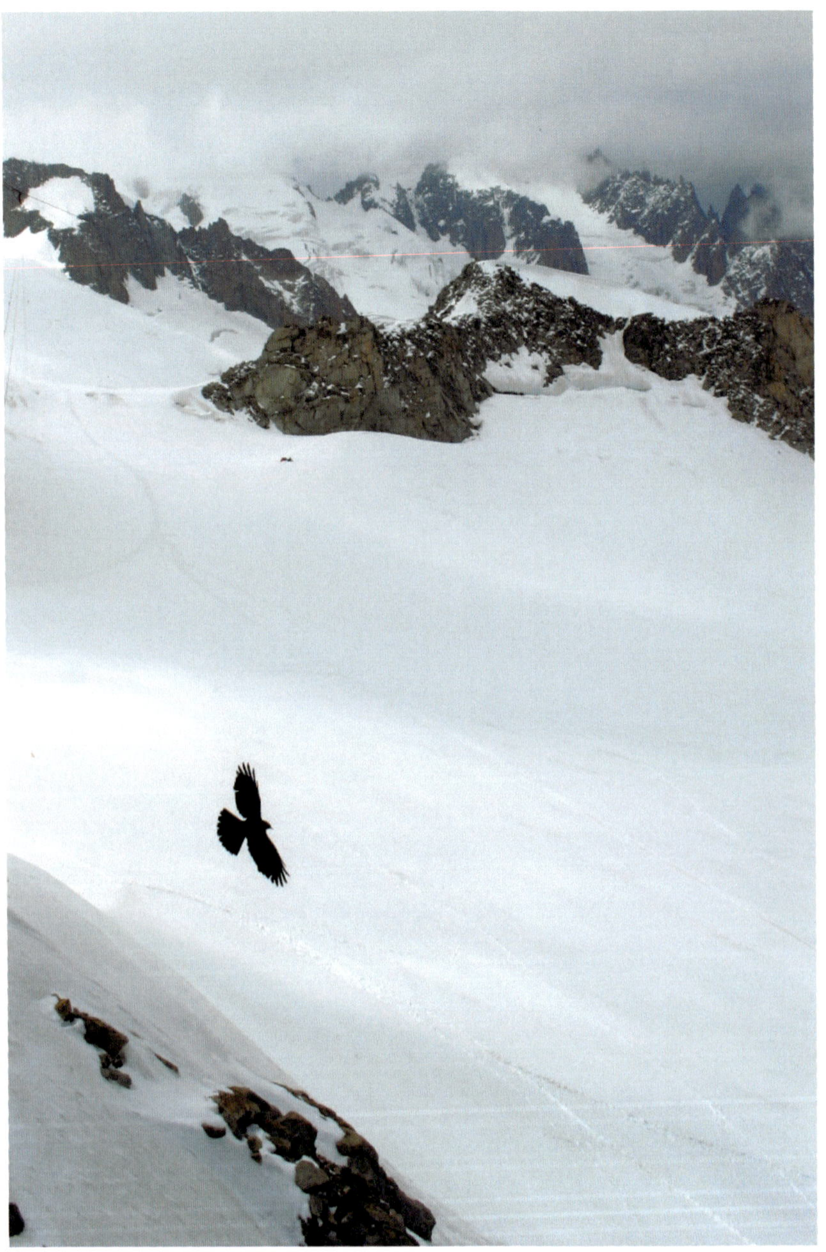

The Raven in the Mist

The steel doors retract.
I glide forward
along Helbronner's Summit,
with my box.
Arcane.
Locked.
Wondering what's inside.

The morning mist beckons.
The wind swells.
But I feel not its breath.

I only can see
a white landscape:
the snowy mountainside,
the frozen observation platform,
the sparkling snowflakes.
One finds its way to my mouth,
but I can't feel it melting on my tongue.

Suddenly I hear
the raven,
flapping his ebony wings,
dancing in the breeze.
"So today is your day," he speaks.

"Mine. In what way?"

"Your journey is at its end."

"I know not how I came to be here. Forgive me if I fear."

"You surely knew this day would come.
All your life
you have prepared
for this very moment."
A rumble of thunder echoed in the distance.
"Do you stand by your choices?" asked the bird.

"Are you saying I'm dead?
This must certainly be a dream
for never have I conversed
with a parrot or cockatoo, much less a raven."

"You have heard birds your whole life," the raven said.
"Now give me the box
and you may proceed through the mist."

"Please tell me," I said.
"What's inside?"

The raven blinked his unblinking eyes, and told me I would be granted
one more choice
if I named the contents of this box.

"What choice would that be?"

"To ride the gondola back to familiar lands,
or to travel forward beyond the mountain
to a place you've never been."

His proposition I contemplated.
The gondola swayed.
Pewter clouds floated by.

"Before you decide, you must ask yourself: 'What is it that I really want?'
Does your box hold your earthly bones and flesh,
or the things you prized most,
or perhaps all of your memories of the material world?"

His misstep—or I think it was so—
was inviting my mind
to roam the abstract realm.
The answer arrived in a flash—
For held bound within that etched box
was all that had impeded me,
those things that created a chasm
between what was and what could have been,
the trepidations that hindered me,
the limitations I perceived in what was possible,
and the fear of what tomorrow might bring.

Smoke issued from the raven's mouth,
and he erupted into flames,
as the lid of the box opened.
Alone once again,
I made my decision
and I began to move....

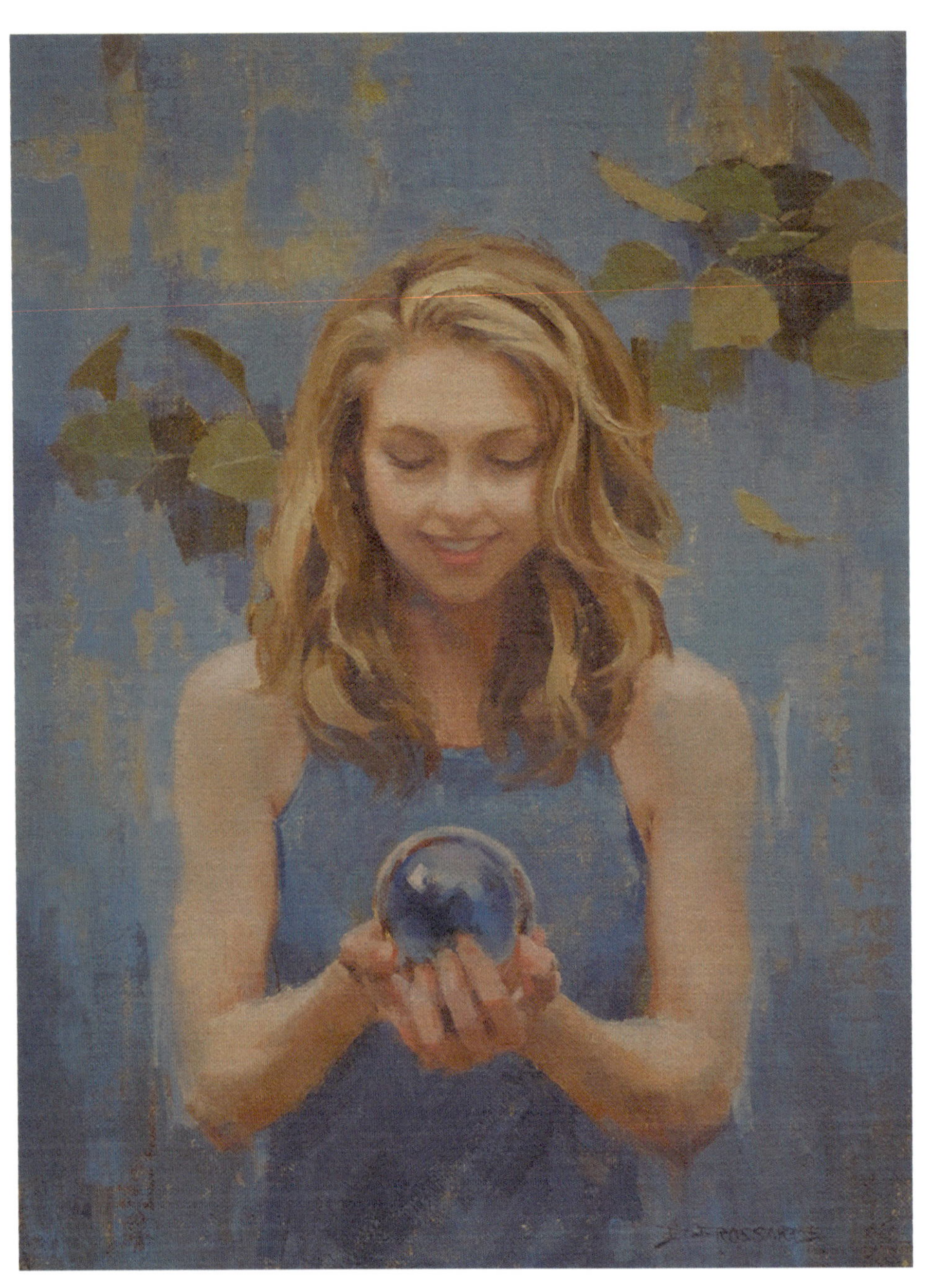

3

In the Meadow

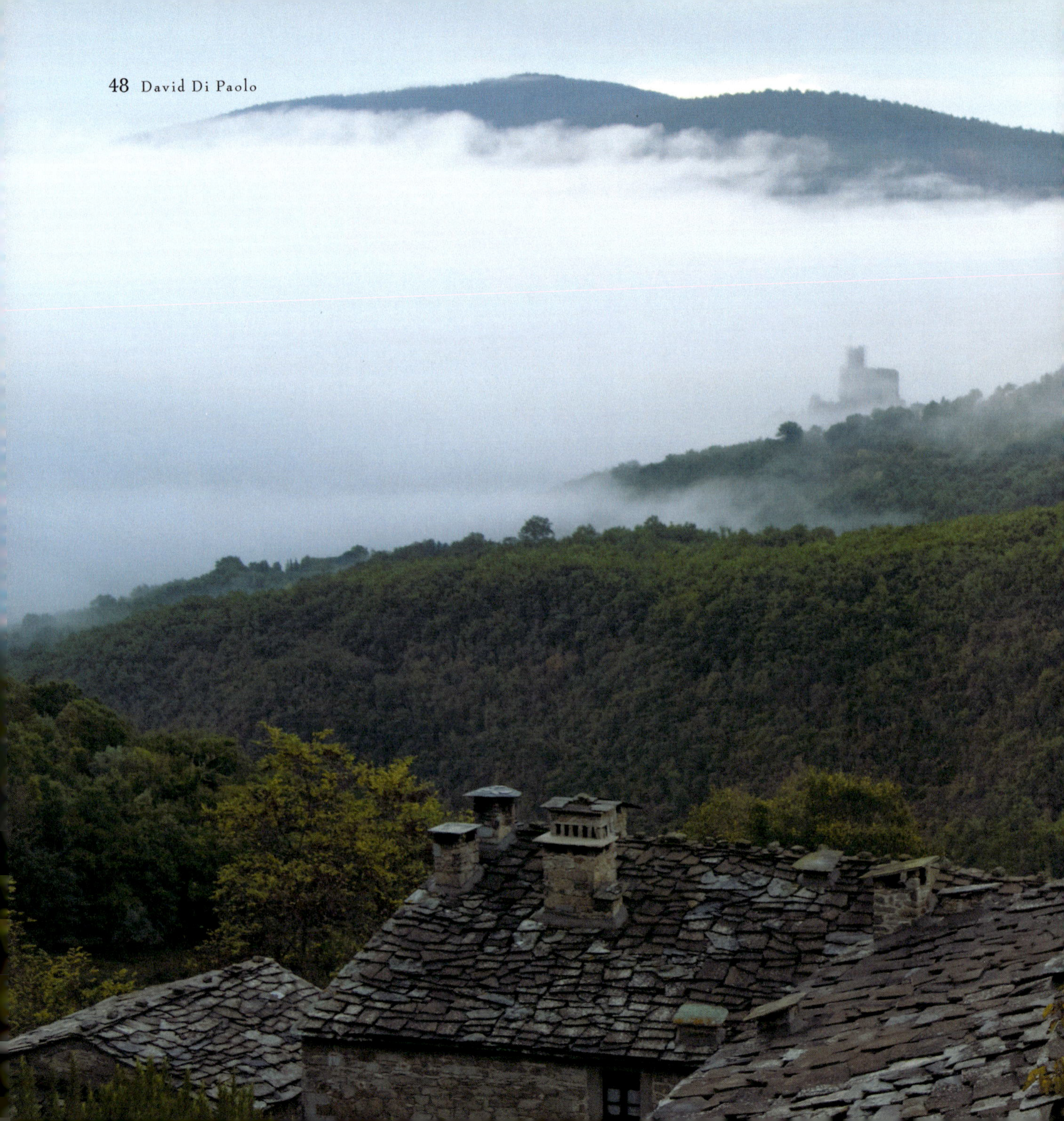

Sunday Morning

Beneath the pergola,
interwoven with vines,
crowned with jewels,
lavender winds
carry their scent
to the olive leaves,
flickering like quicksilver
as they scatter the rays of the Tuscan sun.

The morning fog
lifts its spirit
from the valley below the crumbling tower of Castello di Pierle,
unveiling the dew-covered leaves
of the pregnant fig trees,
while in the distance,
the white dust rises like smoke
behind the spinning wheels of a humming Vespa,
zipping along the strada bianca,
which rims the hill that hides Cortona.

The cement tabletop
kisses my elbows with its cool,
and my hands warm from the heat
of the mug they embrace.

With a long sip of cappuccino,
I accept Dawn's invitation to another Etruscan day,
so happy to be in time with this place
on a wondrous Sunday morn.

The Pea Plant

The chrysalis rises.
The carapace cracks.
Emerge the leaves that take flight,
the harlequin Monarch,
tethered to the ground
by its translucent stem.

A script within,
a performance about to begin,
the final act unwritten.

Lo!
Beware your foes!
Grow tall and firm you must,
before you are bitten.

In you is promise,
hope for tomorrow,
life renewed,
resurrection.

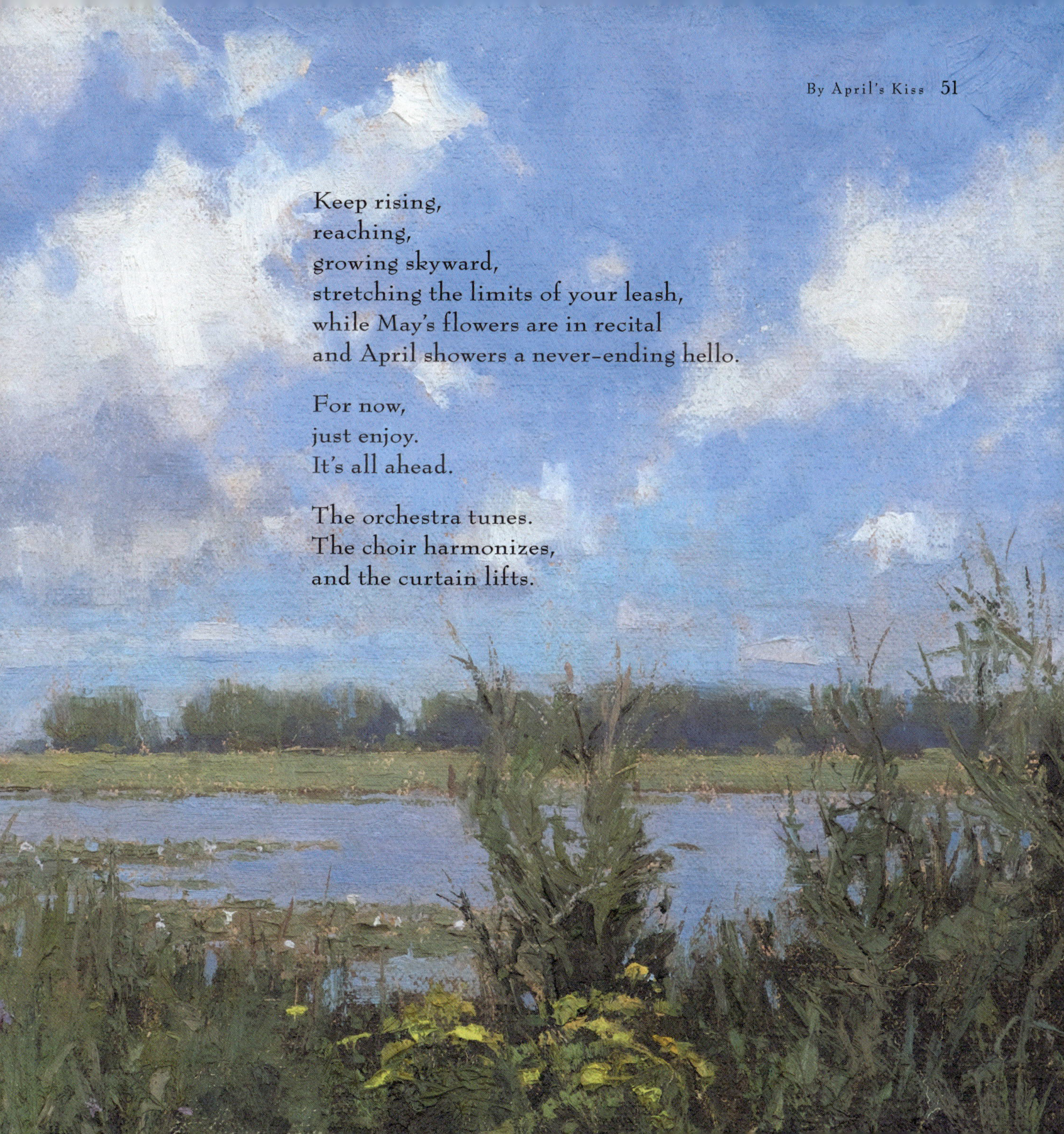

Keep rising,
reaching,
growing skyward,
stretching the limits of your leash,
while May's flowers are in recital
and April showers a never-ending hello.

For now,
just enjoy.
It's all ahead.

The orchestra tunes.
The choir harmonizes,
and the curtain lifts.

White Lily

Every moment is present.
Every second is joy.
When it's you I hold.
Love fills my lungs and surges through my veins.

The future and the past
are faraway shadows
in this blissful daylight that bathes me.

Your smile, it glows …
Your hair, it flows …
I'm fully alive,
when your gaze meets mine.

The past and future,
they do not exist
in this eternal embrace.

A gift from above,
brought by a dove …
My life has never meant more
than when you came to be.

My calla lily,
my white Easter lily,
my daughter, Lily.

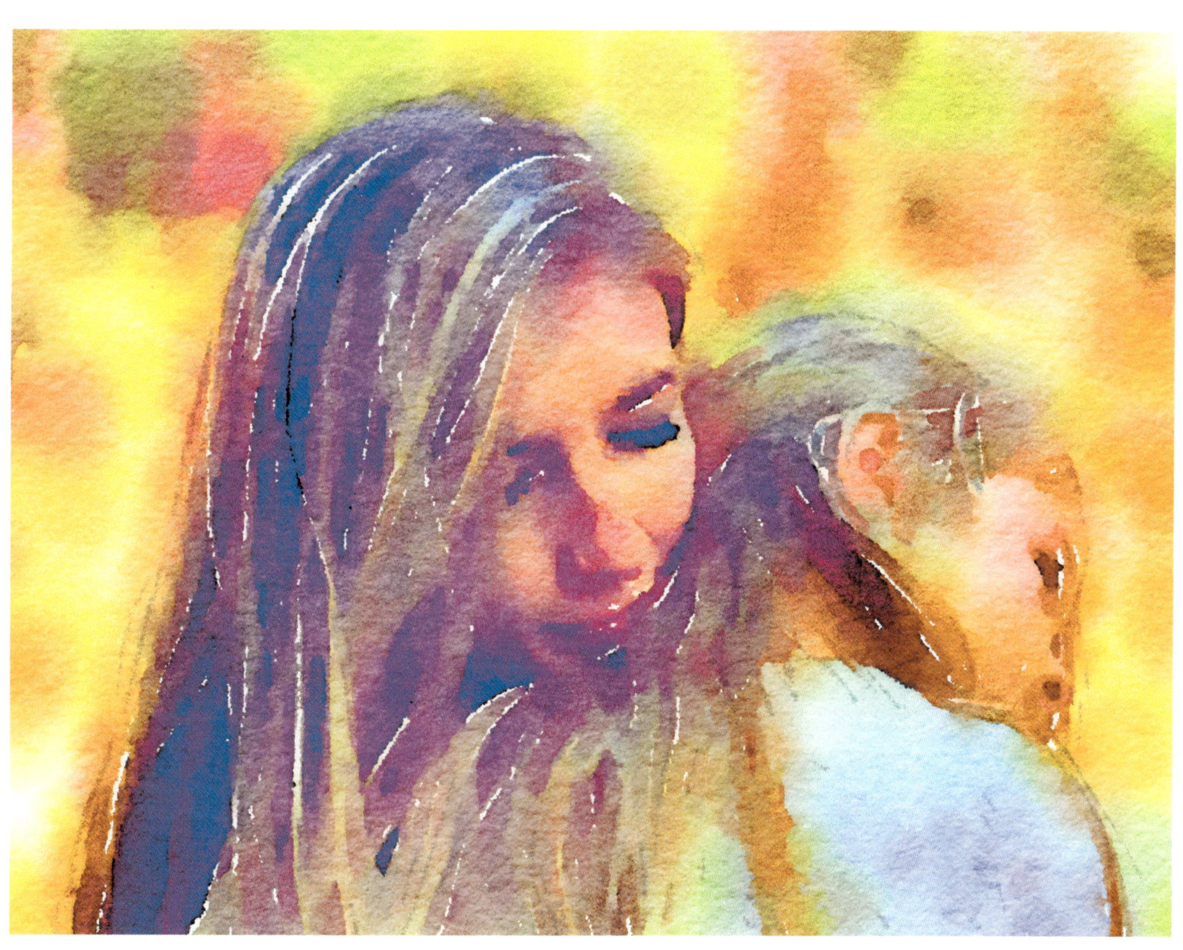

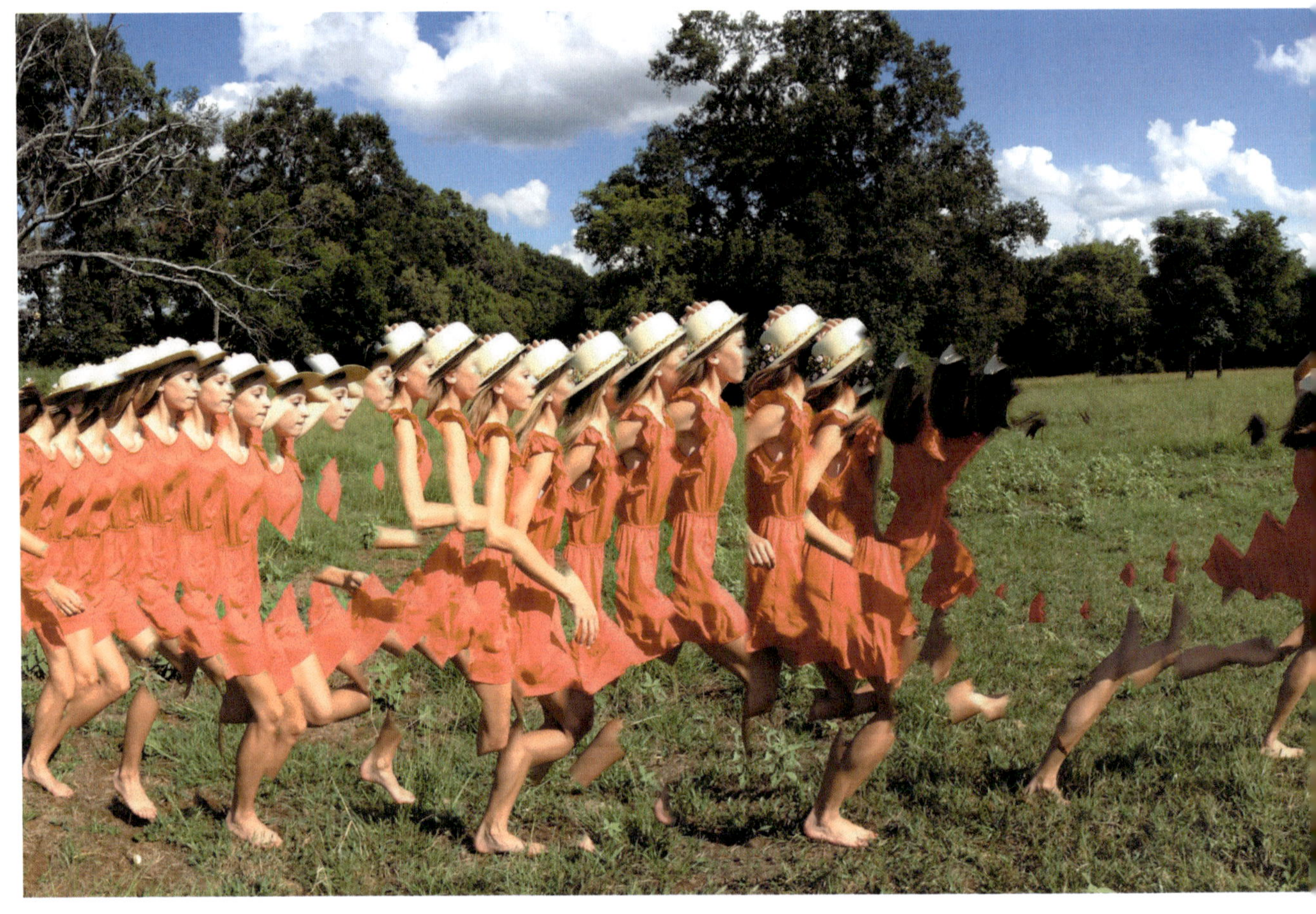

Let's Go on a Picnic

In a meadow of green, kissed with gold,
where the breeze never ceases to whisper,
and the sun banishes the storm clouds.
Afternoon is eternity.

Little Sirena clasps buttercup stems,
daisies sprouting from her woven hair,
while her brothers chase elusive butterflies.
Childhood is eternal.

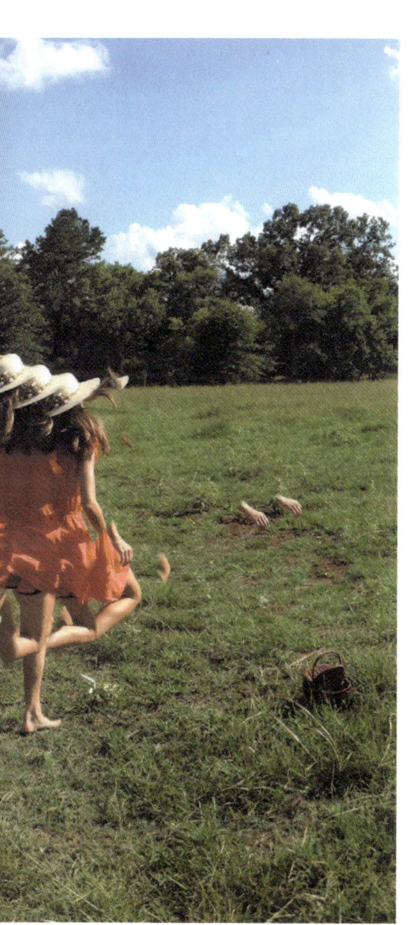

Crescents of watermelon sleep in a bowl,
and slices of lemon float in tumblers,
condensation creeping down the sides,
destined for the checkered blanket
shading fragile blades of grass.
Afternoon is mesmerizing.

The stream sets the rhythm.
The birds provide the melody
to the pastoral song,
whose chorus of silent joy is felt deep within,
during an eternal afternoon.

The basket never empties.
The loaves of bread magically multiply,
and the breeze never ceases to whisper,
"Tomorrow."
The sun may call for a shower and a rainbow,
but today,
there is only a perfect picnic.

Wonder

As I read of the Knights
of the Table Round,
it was you
whose voice was the sound
of a world of wonder
sat atop a mound.

Gold,
silver,
springing from the ground,
to erupt into a crystal cavern
where Galahad,
Lancelot,
and Ewain
surely can be found

The Grail I see,
Excalibur I grasp,
when your voice fills the air.
Legends are alive,
daydreams find purpose.

From mountaintops far apart,
there is a shared vision,
where youth seems forever young,
and the mountain's majesty will never yield.

Charm,
Mystery,
and Melancholy
hold hands
while they circle the maypole.
The leaves of the Aspen trees
shimmy up above,
and you twirl as you sing
enchanting melodies.

Though I never can forget
that one day the snow will fall.

In a vacant A-frame,
I keep gazing out the window,
my novel of the knights' adventures
nestles on the pillow,
while the turntable spins.
The moment approaches
when those who pale in your shadow
follow your steps,
never wanting to go home.

The Last Arrow

I am the voice in the wind that rattles the leaves;
the branch that scrapes your cheek as you meander the forest trails;
the mist that fills the valley;
the jackdaw that sounds overhead;
the chill of morning's frost.

Gaze out the window:
See the sole surviving acorn dangle from the great oak.
Loose one last arrow,
and where the shaft pierces the earth,
mark my remains.
But my spirit lives on.

Legends are we
in the hearts of those who believe
in freedom and justice,
for rich and for poor,
for tall and for small.
Outlaws? No, we never intended to be.

May the sound
of a chorus of merry men
rise from the greenwood,
as the mugs are raised
and the Rhenish ale downed.

I am the hope you seek;
the memory that never fades;
the tickle that wakes you,
that summons your courage,
that gives you purpose.

So abandon your misgivings,
your forgotten trinkets and things.
Rise up from your mat anew.
Take hold of your quarterstaff,
and answer the call
of my blaring sheep's horn,
for you are legend, too.

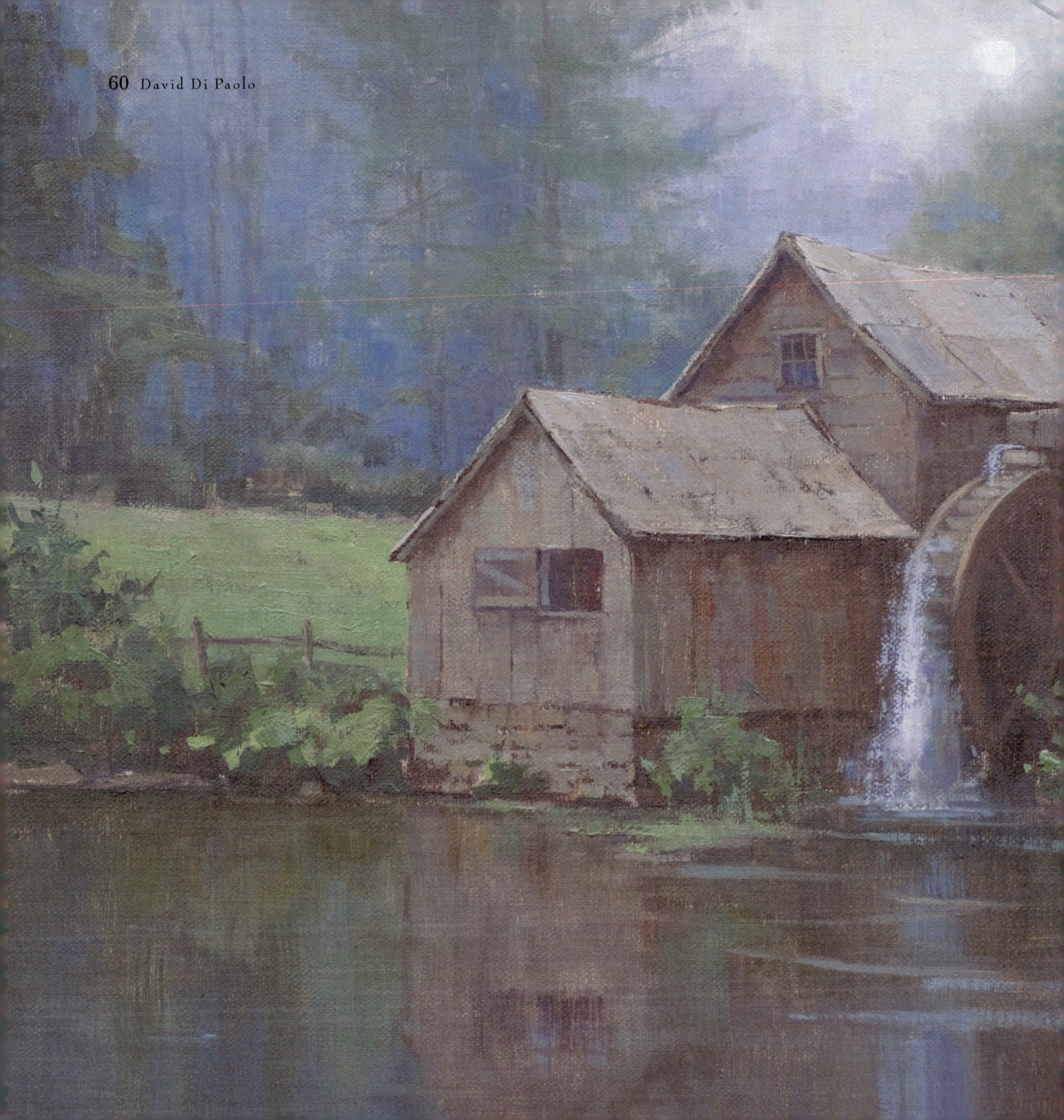

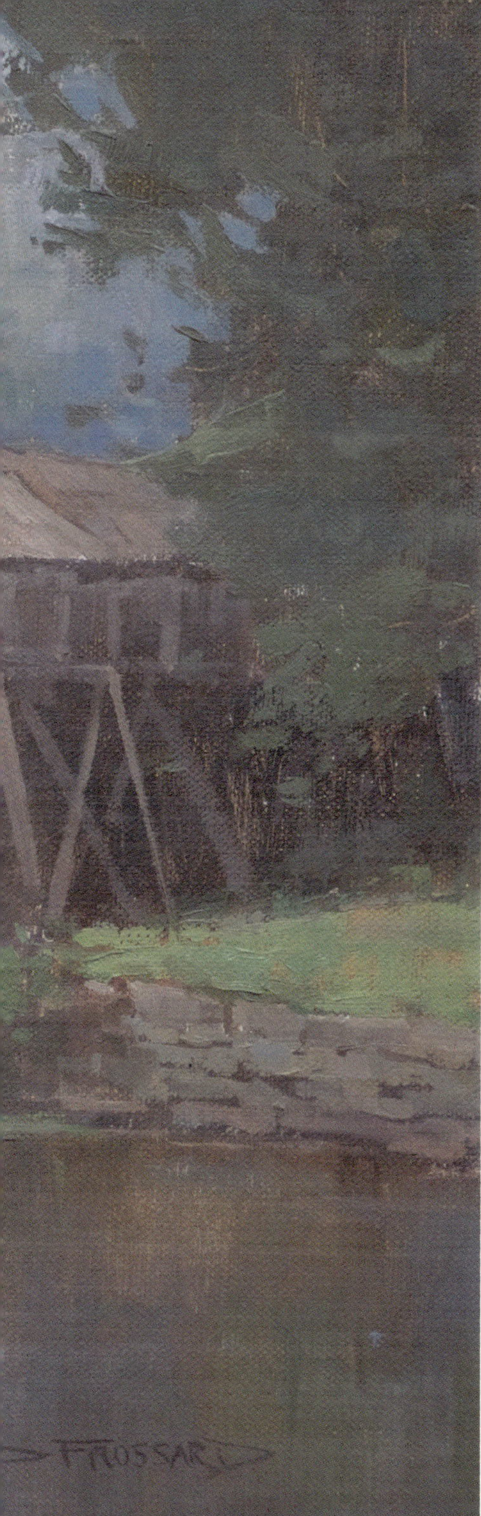

The Watermill

Measuring out possibility,
pouring it forth in sequential bursts,
providing for our livelihood.

Beauty dwells in your labor,
timelessness in your rotations,
personality in your tempo.

Our tireless child,
you never cease
to make us proud.

You've made the barren fields bountiful,
channeled purpose from the streams,
unified a people,
and founded a village.

You are amity, unity,
harmony.

Bottled Sunshine

If only I could bottle,
the essence of your smile.

The upturned corners
of your impish grin
lift the sorrow
lurking far within.

Something about your gaze
puts me in a blissful daze.

The enchanting sparkle
from your mercury eyes
vanquishes the moody darkness
that my evil shadow supplies.

All I see is light.
All I feel warmth.
The clouds genuflect.
The sun takes its throne.
For the sky responds,
when your smile is shone.

Fill this glass
I hold high,
drop by drop.
Displace the liquid malaise fermenting within.

Though I could be wealthy
beyond belief,
if this intoxicant I sold—
I am the richer
for reserving it for myself.

But no,
your essence is not meant to be stoppered.
Let me be the mirror
that reflects the radiance that you bring.
Your light,
your smile
and the overwhelming sense of spring.

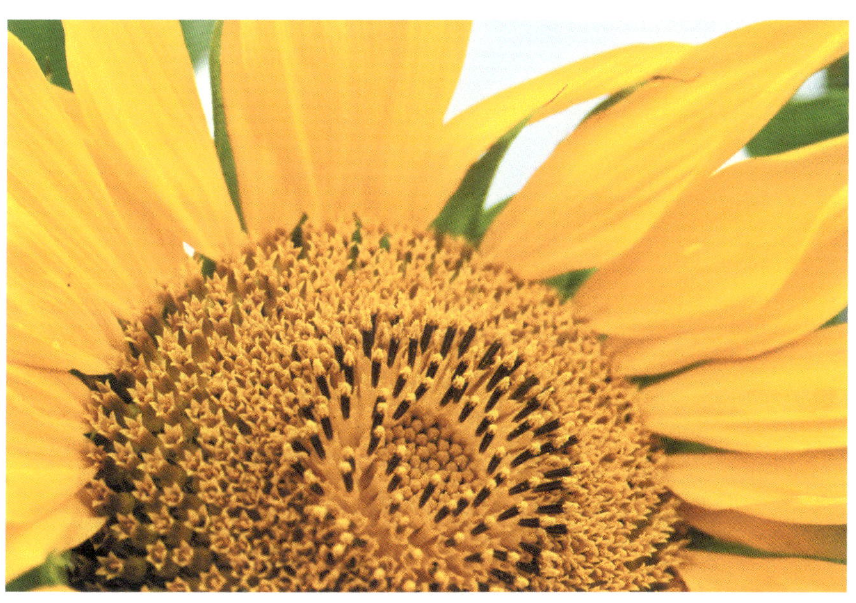

Dragonfly

Circling me.
Calling.
Beckoning
with your playful flight.
Can I heed your message?
Transformation.

You're unlikely courier, sage, and exemplar,
so unusual you are.
So bright,
richly orange.
Are you really just a dragonfly?

I am mesmerized,
tasting the fruit of your light,
feeling the warmth of your glow,
divining the thoughts humming in your wings.
It's not a mirage, a feeling, a superstition.
It's a vision.
A calling.
So I'll answer:
"O river nymph,
what is love?
Can a jaded one trapped beneath the ice
rise above?"

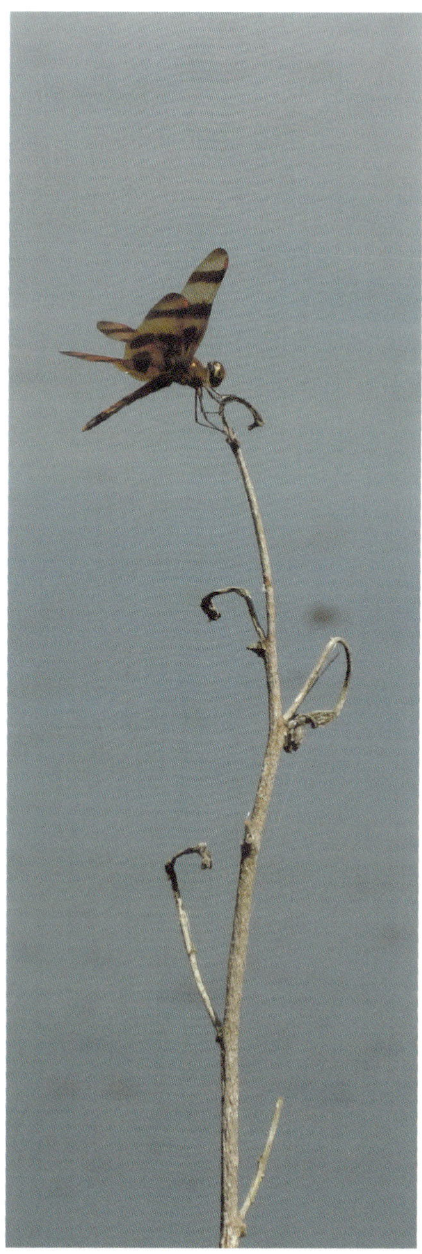

Sunshine
Shine on
Shine on you

Sunshine
Shine on
Shine on me

Sunshine
Shine on
Eternally

Sunshine
Shine forth
Shine the way

Sunshine
Fill me
Give me purpose

Show me
Show me
The way to go

Lead me
Deliver me
Finding freedom

See what I was
Hear what I am
Feel what I can be

Project your thoughts
Your energy
Your knowledge

Enlighten me
With love
Let me believe

Fuse me with your knowledge.
Transform me with your love.

The Wind

The light.
My soul.

The breath.
My spirit.

The thoughts.
My mind.

Calm,
serene.
I am Sea.

Passion,
energy.
I am Flame.

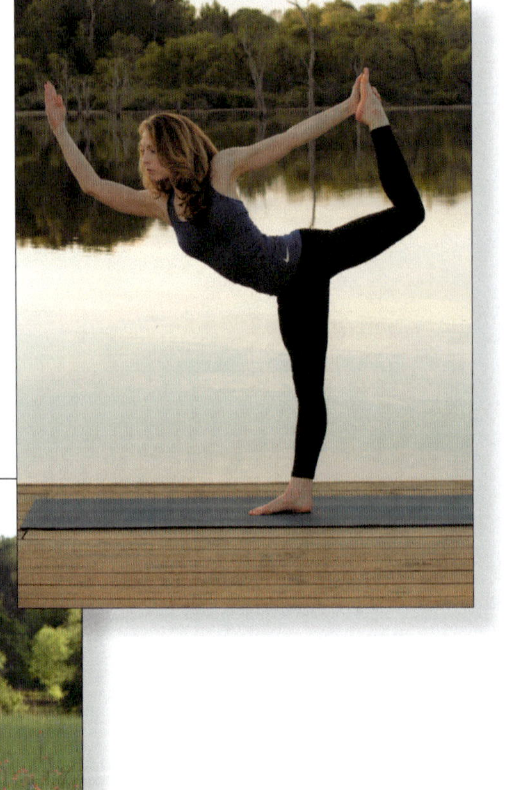

Solid,
steady
I am Rock.

In this moment,
Infinity.
In the next,
Possibility.
In the last,
Memory.

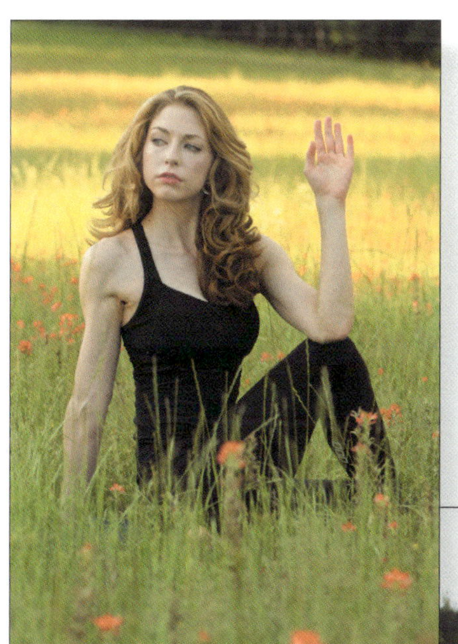

In my breath:
Life.
In my breath:
Spirit.
In my wind:
Consciousness.

Let Me Not Be Vexed

A hand not taken.
A smile not reciprocated.
An embrace not partaken.
A kiss not requited.
A moment not shared.
Let these things be the markers of what should vex me.

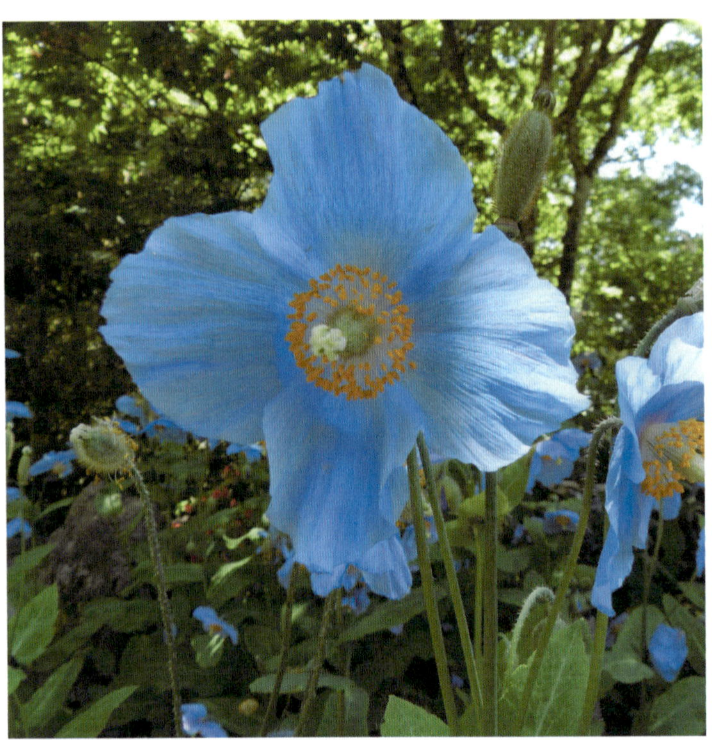

Psalm 151

You gave me bread before I was hungry,
drink before I was thirsty.

The forest,
so I could escape into seclusion,
and discover what was hidden within.

By the setting sun,
I understand the stars I didn't make.

You gave me cause and effect,
so I could reason.

The mountains,
so I could lie in the fog,
clinging to the valley.

The blizzard,
so that I could feel the chill
of the snow that buried me.

By morning's light,
I understand the seasons.

You gave me peace
that I might function.

The ocean,
so I could hear the roar of your voice
in the crashing of the waves.

By the ring around the moon,
I know the storm comes soon.

You gave me survival,
that I have purpose.

Death,
so that we could evolve.

By playing the game,
I've intuited the rules.
By performing in the theater,
I've learned my part.
By riding the wave,
I've made it to shore.
By diving deep,
I've come up for air.

Waves have become
dots have become
letters have become
words have become code.

A plan as it was now is then and ever shall have been.

You kept me company when I was lonely,
offered hope when I despaired.
By the howling wind,
I know I'm no longer alone.

You gave me insight when all was dark,
lucidity when all seemed lost.

The puddle,
to see my reflection
clearly above the mud.

By the shimmering light,
I know the love that could have been ignored.
The love
that might have been forgotten;
the love
that gushes forth from dayspring,
perfusing the atmosphere,
and filling our souls.

Jellyfish

I have this dream,
a strange dream:
I'm drifting;
floating up and sinking down
in a blue lagoon.

The sun glistens
through the sea's undulating ceiling.
A coral jungle beneath my feet.
Somewhere above, a tropical breeze.

I'm so content
to be in this underwater paradise,
my limbs dangling.
So calm.
So peaceful.
Just swaying with the waves,
with my jellyfish clan.
Nowhere to go.
Nothing to do,
except to be in this moment.
And the one after.
So aware of the present,
and without a care
Transparent.

Nothing matters but to be
doing what I was called to do.
Just being.
Aware.
Mindful,
and full of life
Drifting, but always sensing.
And never in flight.

I Can

I *can* make it better.
The composition holds promise,
but it gropes for a guiding hand.
The subject pleads for a touch more focus,
and I must reconsider my perspective.

Couldn't the background have been better envisioned?
Should not the lighting be more dynamic?
Did I not let my complacence
mar her cheek with a distracting sheen?

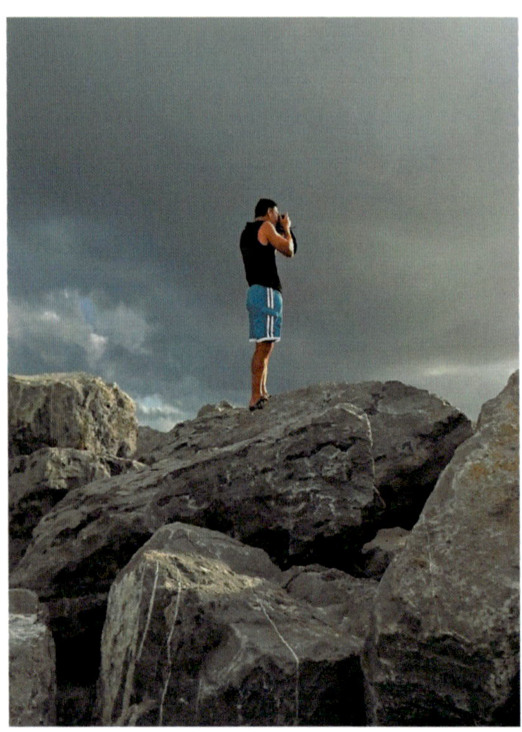

The picture I spy through the viewfinder
is not that which I imagine it could be.
It is an ordinary seed,
but one from which
we will make magic sprout.

Lend me your hand,
and let us balance on the shoulders of giants,
who have shared their wisdom.
Let us find life
and discover the promise latent in this image.

With your help,
I'm ready to venture forth,
leave the darkroom and studio,
and enter the light of day.
Let me unholster my camera
And uncap the lens.

I'm about to make it better,
Better for me.
Better for you.
Better for the world my camera and I behold.

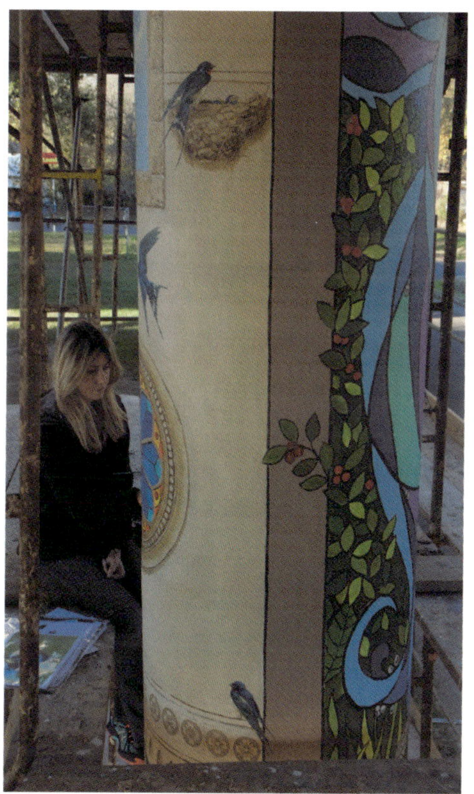

Acknowledgments

I am indebted to my wife, Susan, for her resolute support and constant encouragement. Special thanks to Diane Frossard, artist and friend. Although I didn't think it possible, I enjoyed our collaboration for this project even more than for our first team effort, *The Artemis Connection*. Models who offered their time, expressions, and vitality include: Kelly Frossard, Hannah Frossard, Emily Dallas, Lilyan Cooper, and Taylor Clark. Grazie mille to Anna Pritchard, who reviewed the rough draft of the manuscript and helped me past early stumbling blocks in the writing process.

I would also like to express my gratitude to Lisa Schleipfer, developmental editor, who helped refine passages and focus the concept of the piece; thank you to Howard Johnson, designer, for lending his expertise and creative input; as well as Lisa Akoury-Ross, owner of SDP Publishing Solutions, LLC, for her guidance and encouragement.

Lastly, I'd like to express my gratitude to Grace Knight, who prompted me to write descriptive passages and poems, by requesting that I contribute to her book of poetry, *The Tangles of Life*, a work inspired by her personal struggles coping with cystic fibrosis. In the face of a disease that grants no quarter, Grace has an unyielding optimism, and she is a boundless source of inspiration.

Illustration & Photo Credits

(images are listed in order of appearance in the book)

Book cover & Illustration 1 – *By the Creek*	Diane Frossard
Photo 1 – *Dandelion & Sky*	David Di Paolo
Illustration 2 – *Moon Reflections*	Diane Frossard
Photo 2 – *Foggy Field*	Diane Frossard
Photo 3 – *Lonely Trail*	Diane Frossard
Photo 4 – *White Rose*	David Di Paolo
Photo 5 – *Commute*	David Di Paolo
Photo 6 – *Crystal Ball*	David Di Paolo
Illustration 3 – *Hannah*	Diane Frossard
Photo 7 – *Winter*	David Di Paolo
Photo 8 – *Foggy Morning*	Diane Frossard
Photo 9 – *Time Passing*	David Di Paolo
Photo 10 – *Lavender Rose*	David Di Paolo
Photo 11 – *Untitled 227*	David Di Paolo
Photo 12 – *Mont Blanc Raven*	David Di Paolo
Illustration 4 & Back Cover – *Tomorrow Today*	Diane Frossard
Photo 13 – *Borgo di Vagli*	David Di Paolo

Illustration 5 – *Crex Meadows*	Diane Frossard
Photo 14 – *Emily & Lily*	David Di Paolo
Photo 15 – *Saturday Afternoon*	David Di Paolo
Photo 16 – *Tuscan Field*	David Di Paolo
Illustration 6 – *Watermill*	Diane Frossard
Photo 17 – *Sunflower*	David Di Paolo
Photo 18 – *Dragonfly*	Diane Frossard
Photo 19 – *Flame*	David Di Paolo
Photo 20 – *Rock*	David Di Paolo
Photo 21 – *Free*	David Di Paolo
Photo 22 – *Sea*	David Di Paolo
Photo 23 – *Blue Poppy*	David Di Paolo
Photo 24 – *Lion King*	Diane Frossard
Photo 25 – *Pillar of Hope*	David Di Paolo
Author photo	Ron Ragan
Artist photo	Fran Ellisor

About the Author

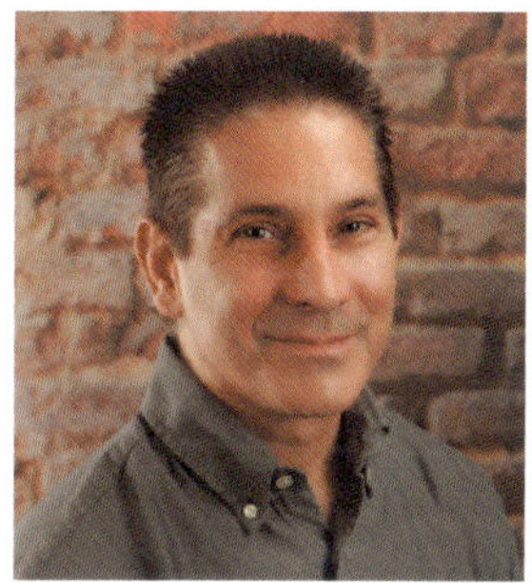

Author of the Magical Realism novel, *The Artemis Connection*, David Di Paolo also has written scripts for medical segments airing on the television evening news, contributed fitness articles to the *Tyler Morning Telegraph*, and authored a wellness blog for BSCENE.com. He is a physician and photographer, providing many of the images for this publication. This is his second book.

About the Artist

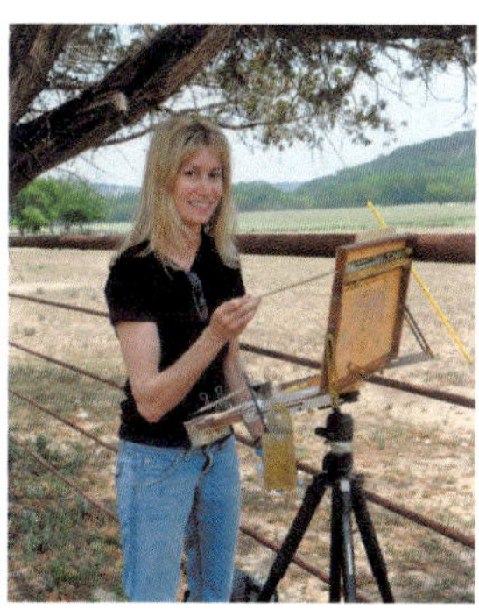

A lifetime artist, Diane Ditzler Frossard has a passion for both portrait work and plein-air painting. Her focus is on the effects of light and dynamic design—rather than a specific subject—striving to go beyond documentation, capturing the mood and beauty of a unique moment in time and creating a visual poem. Her daughters Hannah and Kelly served as models for some of the artwork in this book. Diane's website is http://dianefrossard.com.

CPSIA information can be obtained at www.ICGtesting.com
Printed in the USA
LVIW01n2254110417
530491LV00001B/2